MEDITATION AND MENTAL WELL BEING

THE PATH TO INNER PEACE AND CLARITY

DR. MINAKSHI BANSAL

Made with ♥ on the Notion Press Platform
www.notionpress.com

Dedication

This book is dedicated to all seekers of peace and clarity—those who have embarked on the journey of self-discovery through meditation and those who are poised to begin. To the novices who are curious and eager, to the experienced practitioners who continue to explore the depths of their minds, and to everyone in between: may this guide serve as a beacon on your path.

To my family and friends, for their unwavering support and patience through my own journey in meditation, and to my mentors and teachers, whose wisdom and guidance have illuminated my way, this book is also for you.

Lastly, this book is dedicated to the quiet moments of reflection, the deep breaths of resolve, and the gentle steps toward greater mindfulness and compassion in a world that needs it more than ever.

▷▷▷

Contents

Contents

Prayer

"Om Bhadram Karnebhih Shrinuyama Devah
Bhadram Pashyemakshabhiryajatrah
Sthirairangais Tushtuvamsastanubhih
Vyashema Devahitam Yadayuh
Svasti Na Indro Vriddhashravah
Svasti Nah Pusha Vishwavedah
Svasti Nastarkshyo Arishtanemih
Svasti No Brihaspatir Dadhatu
Om Shantih Shantih Shantih"

This mantra is a prayer for universal well-being, invoking the blessings of various deities for protection, health, and happiness. It emphasizes the importance of experiencing the auspicious through all senses and living a life aligned with divine purpose. The repetition of "Shantih" at the end signifies a deep desire for peace in the individual, the environment, and the universe at large. This mantra is often recited as a prayer for peace, prosperity, and the physical and spiritual well-being of all beings.

About The Author

Dr. Minakshi Bansal, born in the bustling metropolis of Delhi, India, has led a life steeped in artistry, scholarly pursuit, and an unwavering commitment to societal betterment. Following her marriage, she relocated to Ahmedabad, Gujarat, where she has since blossomed into a multifaceted beacon of inspiration for many. Dr. Minakshi is not only recognized as a gifted artist in the realm of Fine Arts but also as an esteemed author, a devoted social worker and a dedicated research scholar in Psychology. Her journey, marked by a profound dedication to elevating those around her, especially the downtrodden and underprivileged children of society, is a testament to her deep-seated belief in the transformative power of engagement and empathy.

From her earliest days, Minakshi was distinguished by an insatiable appetite for reading. Her literary universe was inhabited by characters and narratives that spanned ethical tales, motivational and inspirational stories, and the mythic parables imbued with life lessons. This voracious reading habit was not merely for personal edification but was driven by a desire to distill and disseminate the essence of these narratives to foster the development of students and peers alike. She was particularly captivated by the lives and teachings of historical figures and spiritual leaders such as Adi Shankaracharya, Swami Vivekananda, Dr. APJ Abdul Kalam, Mahamana Pandit Madan Mohan Malviya, Mahatma Gandhi, Sardar Vallabhai Patel, and Vinoba Bhave, among others. Their philosophies and life stories fueled her ambition to embody their ideals of resilience, selflessness, and relentless pursuit of knowledge.

Dr. Minakshi's academic and practical engagement with psychology has been equally noteworthy. As a research scholar, her focus has been on exploring the intricate tapestry of the human psyche, aiming to unlock the potential for psychological well-being and societal harmony. Her scholarly work is complemented by her active involvement in social work, where she employs her academic insights to make tangible differences in the lives of the underprivileged. Her endeavours in social work are characterized by an innovative approach that combines traditional wisdom with contemporary psychological practices to address the multifaceted challenges faced by these communities.

Her artistic talents, another facet of her diverse capabilities, are not merely a personal passion but also serve as a medium through which she communicates and connects with others. Her art, rich in symbolism and emotional depth, reflects her philosophical inquiries and social concerns, offering viewers a glimpse into the breadth of her intellect and the depth of her compassion.

In addition to her contributions to the arts and social sciences, Dr. Minakshi has embraced the healing arts of Pranic Healing, mastering the techniques developed by Master Choa Kok Sui. This practice, which focuses on the manipulation of Prana or life energy to heal the body and aura, has been both a personal journey of discovery and a means through which she extends her healing touch to others. Her proficiency in Pranic Healing is complemented by her advocacy and teaching of various forms of meditation aimed at rejuvenation, personal betterment, and the cultivation of harmony within individuals and communities alike.

Dr. Minakshi's life is a narrative of relentless pursuit, not just of personal achievement but of the upliftment and empowerment of society at large. Her diverse interests and talents—spanning the arts, literature, psychology, and the healing practices—converge on a singular path of service. She embodies the spirit of the luminaries who inspired her, channelling their legacy through her actions and teachings. Through her books, art, and social initiatives, she continues to inspire a new generation to embark on their own journeys of self-discovery, resilience, and altruism.

Her commitment to social betterment, particularly her focus on uplifting underprivileged children, reflects a deep understanding of the transformative potential of education and personal development. By integrating her knowledge of psychology, her artistic sensibilities, and her healing practices, Dr. Bansal has developed a holistic approach to social work that addresses both the immediate needs and the long-term well-being of the communities she serves.

As an author, Dr. Minakshi's writings offer a blend of inspirational insights, practical wisdom, and reflective contemplations drawn from her extensive reading and life experiences. Her books serve as a guide for those seeking to navigate the complexities of life with grace, resilience, and purpose. Through her narratives, she extends an invitation to her readers to explore the depths of their own potential and to contribute meaningfully to the collective well-being of society.

In Dr. Minakshi Bansal, we find a remarkable synthesis of the artist, the scholar, the healer, and the social activist. Her life's work stands as a beacon of hope and a source of inspiration for individuals seeking to make a difference in the world. Her story is a compelling reminder of the power of individual action, rooted in compassion and driven by a profound commitment to the betterment of humanity. Dr. Minakshi's legacy is not just in the tangible outcomes of her efforts but in the enduring spirit of inquiry, empathy, and service that she embodies.

ppp

Preface

The journey to inner peace and clarity is a quest as ancient as humanity itself. In our modern world, filled with constant noise and myriad distractions, the need for a centered existence has never been more pressing. This book is born out of this necessity—a guide designed to help you navigate the complexities of contemporary life through the timeless practice of meditation.

This book is not merely a collection of techniques; it is an invitation to embark on a transformative journey towards a quieter mind and a more fulfilling life. It recognizes meditation as a deeply personal practice but also as a universally accessible tool that can help us manage stress, enhance our relationships, and promote emotional health. Each chapter within this book builds upon the next, creating a comprehensive guide that evolves with you, whether you are a novice just beginning to explore meditation or a seasoned practitioner seeking to deepen your practice.

The idea for this book came to me during a meditation retreat, a serene experience that highlighted the profound impact regular meditation had on my own life. It wasn't just the immediate effects during the sessions that were transformative but how the principles of mindfulness seeped into and enriched every aspect of my day-to-day activities. I left the retreat with a renewed sense of purpose to share these benefits with others, to demystify the practice of meditation, and make it accessible to a broader audience.

In the chapters that follow, you will find a detailed exploration of what meditation is and isn't—an introduction that dispels common myths and outlines the scientific underpinnings that support its benefits. From there, we delve into practical advice for establishing your practice, discussing various types of meditation, and offering tips to integrate these practices into your daily routine.

Recognizing that personal growth occurs within a community context, this book also explores the impact of meditation on relationships and how meditative practices can be adapted for different age groups and life stages. It acknowledges that life's only constant is change and provides strategies to adapt your meditation practice as your life evolves.

Technology, too, plays a crucial role in modern meditation practices. This book examines how digital tools can support and enhance your meditation journey, providing reviews and recommendations on the best apps and online resources available. At the same time, it addresses potential pitfalls in letting technology dominate your practice, advocating for a balanced approach that keeps the focus on mindfulness and personal insight.

Moreover, the text does not shy away from discussing the challenges that often accompany meditation. It offers honest advice on how to overcome common obstacles like restlessness, distraction, and the perceived lack of time—challenges that many face in their meditative practices. Here, you'll find encouragement and strategies to maintain motivation and sustain a lifelong meditation practice that adapts to your changing needs and circumstances.

Throughout this book, personal anecdotes from diverse practitioners enrich the narrative, providing real-world examples of how meditation has improved lives. These stories not only serve to inspire but also illustrate the universal appeal and adaptability of meditation across different cultures, lifestyles, and personal backgrounds.

As you turn the pages, I invite you to approach each chapter with an open mind and a willing heart. Consider this book not just as a reading exercise but as a practical guide to be returned to time and again. Each reading can offer new insights and reinforce your commitment to this life-enhancing practice.

In closing, "Meditation and Mental Well-Being: The Path to Inner Peace and Clarity" is more than just a book; it is a companion on your journey towards a more peaceful and insightful life. It is my hope that through this book, you will discover not just the techniques of meditation but the joy and profound peace that come with a mindful existence. Here's to finding your path to inner peace and clarity, one breath at a time.

Dr. Minakshi Bansal
Social Activist
Ahmedabad, Gujarat, Bharat

ᕹᕹᕹ

ONE
INTRODUCTION TO MEDITATION

Meditation, a practice as ancient as civilization itself, has woven its threads deeply through the fabric of human history, finding its place in the tapestry of various cultures worldwide. At its core, meditation is a deliberate practice that involves turning one's attention away from distracting thoughts to focus on the present moment, often using breath, a sound, or a particular object to guide this focus. Despite its simplicity, the profound impact of meditation on the mind and body is backed by centuries of anecdotal evidence and, more recently, scientific research.

The roots of meditation stretch back to prehistoric times when shamans entered trance states during rituals. However, it was in the ancient Indian scriptures known as the Vedas that meditation first appeared with more structured outlines. The practice permeated various aspects of life and soon spread beyond India, adapting to the cultural nuances of regions from Asia to the Mediterranean.

Buddhism, perhaps more than any other religion, has been instrumental in shaping the practice of meditation. Siddhartha Gautama, the Buddha, used meditation as a means to enlightenment in the 6th century BCE. His teachings outlined mindfulness and concentration techniques that remain central to Buddhist practices today.

As Buddhism spread to countries like China, Japan, and Thailand, each culture infused its meditation practices with local traditions, leading to the development of diverse forms such as Zen in Japan and Vipassana in Thailand.

Similarly, other major religions incorporated forms of meditative practice. In Christianity, contemplative prayer and the repetition of phrases similar to mantras serve as a form of meditation focused on communion with God. Islamic Sufism uses dhikr, the recitation of divine phrases, as a meditative practice to remember and glorify God.

Even in indigenous traditions across the Americas and Africa, meditation-like practices were employed, often in the form of rhythmic chanting and dancing meant to induce trance states for spiritual encounters and community bonding.

In more recent times, meditation has transcended spiritual boundaries to become a resource in health and well-being, thanks in part to a growing body of scientific research that underscores its benefits. Studies have demonstrated that regular meditation can reduce stress, control anxiety, and decrease blood pressure, making it a valuable tool in the management of various physical and psychological conditions.

These benefits are believed to stem from meditation's impact on the brain's plasticity, increasing areas associated with well-being and reducing those linked to stress.

Furthermore, meditation encourages a deep state of relaxation and a tranquil mind, which can lead to enhanced mood, better cognitive function, and overall improved quality of life. For many, these benefits are compelling reasons to incorporate meditation into their daily routines.

Despite these extensive benefits, misconceptions about meditation persist. It is often mistakenly seen as a religious practice, a form of mental exertion, or something that requires special expertise to achieve. In reality, meditation is a secular, accessible practice that does not strive to empty the mind but rather to understand and transform it.

It is not about achieving a superhuman state of concentration but about learning to exist in the present and observe one's thoughts without judgment.

The practice of meditation involves several techniques, each suited to different personality types and lifestyles. For some, focusing on the breath provides the anchor for their practice; for others, repeating a mantra facilitates a deeper state of contemplation.

Techniques vary widely, from mindfulness, which involves paying attention to thoughts as they arise without engagement, to more structured practices like guided meditations, which use verbal instructions to direct the practitioner's imagination or awareness.

Cultural interpretations of meditation also continue to evolve, blending traditional practices with modern needs. For instance, in the fast-paced environment of Western societies, meditation has been adapted to address the specific stresses of contemporary life.

Apps and online courses have proliferated, offering guided sessions that help users meditate for relaxation, sleep better, or enhance productivity. This adaptability underscores meditation's enduring relevance, offering a timeless remedy to the human condition's challenges.

Meditation offers a profound simplicity that belies its transformative power. From ancient spiritual rituals to modern health practices, it has consistently provided a means for deeper self-awareness and enhanced well-being. As we continue to navigate the complexities of modern life, meditation remains a vital tool, inviting us to pause, breathe, and align ourselves with the present moment.

This ancient practice not only enriches our personal lives but also deepens our understanding of the cultures that have shaped it, highlighting our shared human heritage and the universal quest for peace and clarity.

ϼϼϼ

"Meditation is the art of mastering the mind through the stillness of the body. In those quiet moments, we discover not only who we are, but also who we might become. It is the journey from noise to silence, from chaos to calm."

❥❥❥

TWO

THE SCIENCE OF MEDITATION

Meditation, once the realm of mystics and monks, has now become a common household practice, recognized for its profound benefits on mental and physical health. This widespread acceptance is largely due to decades of scientific research that have explored and validated the positive effects of meditation. Through various studies, scientists have been able to map out how regular meditation can not only alleviate symptoms of stress and anxiety but also improve overall well-being and even enhance certain cognitive functions.

The journey into the scientific exploration of meditation began in earnest in the latter half of the 20th century. Researchers were curious about anecdotal reports that meditation could reduce stress and increase focus. One of the pioneering studies in this field was conducted by Dr. Herbert Benson of Harvard University in the 1970s. He discovered what he called the "relaxation response," a physical state of deep rest that changes the physical and emotional responses to stress. Benson's work showed that meditation could reduce traits commonly associated with stress such as hypertension, heart rate, and breathing problems.

Further research has expanded on these findings to explore various types of meditation, including mindfulness meditation, transcendental meditation, and focused attention meditation, among others. Each style has its unique method and benefits, but they all share a common goal: to bring the mind to a state of calm awareness.

One of the most significant areas of interest has been the effect of meditation on the brain. Neuroscientific research using tools like MRI (Magnetic Resonance Imaging) has shown that meditation can lead to changes in brain structure—something once thought impossible after a certain age. For instance, a notable study published by researchers at Massachusetts General Hospital found that eight weeks of mindfulness-based stress reduction (MBSR) led to an increase in the cortical thickness in the hippocampus, which governs learning and memory, and in certain areas of the brain that play roles in emotion regulation and self-referential processing.

These changes in brain structure correspond with improvements in function. For example, regular meditators often report better attention and concentration, and these reports are backed by research. Studies have found that meditation enhances the brain's ability to process information quickly and manage tasks without getting distracted. This makes it an excellent tool for combating the effects of age-related cognitive decline as well as improving younger individuals' academic and professional performances.

Meditation's impact on mental health is equally profound. Numerous studies have demonstrated its efficacy in reducing symptoms of anxiety and depression. This is thought to occur through meditation's ability to improve regulation of the "fight or flight" system in the brain, with less reactive and more controlled responses to stress. By reducing chronic stress, meditation helps to mitigate the effects of anxiety and depression, offering a complementary tool alongside traditional therapies.

Beyond mental health, meditation has also been found to have tangible physical health benefits. For instance, it has been shown to improve cardiovascular health by reducing blood pressure, which is a major risk factor for heart disease. This is likely due to its ability to help reduce stress hormones, which can constrict blood vessels and increase heart rate.

Furthermore, meditation has been linked to a better immune response. A study conducted by researchers in Wisconsin, Spain, and France reported higher levels of antibodies in flu vaccine recipients who meditated, suggesting that regular meditation might boost the immune system's ability to fight off illnesses.

Another significant area of research has been how meditation can aid in managing pain. Studies have shown that meditators report lower pain sensitivity, and brain imaging studies suggest that meditation contributes to pain management by decreasing brain activity in areas responsible for processing pain sensation. This suggests that meditation can play an essential role in chronic pain management strategies.

Given this vast array of scientific evidence, it is clear why meditation has moved from the fringes to mainstream acceptance as a valuable health tool. It offers a low-cost, low-risk means to significantly enhance both mental and physical health, applicable across various settings—from schools to workplaces to clinical environments. As research continues to deepen our understanding of its benefits, meditation is likely to become even more integrated into everyday health practices, underscoring its importance as a powerful tool in enhancing human health and quality of life.

In sum, the science behind meditation reveals a technique that is not only beneficial for personal well-being but is also powerfully transformative. This body of research has not only validated centuries-old wisdom but has also opened new avenues for using mindfulness and meditation to address complex health issues in the modern world. As we continue to explore the depths of the mind and its impact on the body, meditation stands as a testament to the potential within each individual to foster significant changes through the simple act of sitting quietly and tuning into the rhythm of one's own breath.

ᐯᐯᐯ

"Each breath in meditation is a step towards peace, a silent guide through the chaos of the world. With every inhale, we draw in life; with every exhale, we release what burdens us. Thus, we find balance in the rhythm of our breathing."

ɒɒɒ

THREE

GETTING STARTED WITH MEDITATION

Starting a meditation practice can seem daunting at first, especially if one is unfamiliar with the process. However, meditation is fundamentally a simple practice accessible to everyone, regardless of age, lifestyle, or background. Here, we explore practical advice for beginners, including how to set up a meditation space and how to incorporate meditation into a daily routine.

The first step in beginning a meditation practice is understanding what meditation is: a period of dedicated time to focus inwardly and cultivate mindfulness. The practice doesn't require special equipment or an elaborate setup, making it an accessible tool for enhancing mental and physical well-being.

Choosing a Meditation Space

Selecting a suitable place for meditation is crucial as it can significantly affect how your practice develops. The space doesn't need to be large but should be somewhat secluded and quiet, where interruptions are minimized. It could be a corner of a bedroom, a home office, or even a spot on a comfortable living room chair. The key is consistency; using the same space regularly can help condition the mind to enter a meditative state more readily.

The area should feel peaceful and inviting. Some people like to personalize their meditation space with items that promote a calming atmosphere, such as cushions, a yoga mat, or a small altar with items like candles, incense, or meaningful symbols. The idea is to make the space inviting and conducive to relaxation and introspection.

Scheduling Meditation Time

One of the biggest challenges beginners face is finding time to meditate amidst the hustle and bustle of daily life. Meditation doesn't require hours of commitment; even a few minutes each day can yield significant benefits. Many find that meditating at the same time each day creates a routine that becomes a regular part of their lifestyle. Morning meditation can start the day with a calm, clear mindset, while evening sessions might help unwind and process the day's events.

For those new to meditation, starting with as little as five minutes a day is an excellent way to build a habit. It's more beneficial to meditate for a short time each day than to do longer sessions sporadically. As comfort with the practice grows, gradually increase the time. A timer can be a useful tool to keep track of time without distraction.

Beginning the Practice

With a space set up and a time scheduled, the next step is to begin meditating. Start by sitting comfortably in your chosen spot. You can sit on a chair, cushion, or mat, ensuring your back is straight but not strained. The hands can rest lightly on your knees or in your lap. Close your eyes or keep them slightly open with a soft focus on the ground a few feet in front of you.

Begin by taking several deep breaths, inhaling through the nose and exhaling through the mouth. This helps signal the body to relax and prepare for meditation. Then, let your breathing return to a normal rhythm and start to pay attention to the breath's natural flow. Notice the sensation of air entering and leaving your nostrils, or the rise and fall of your chest or abdomen.

When your mind wanders, as it inevitably will, gently acknowledge the thoughts and then refocus on your breath. This redirection of attention back to the breath is the heart of mindfulness meditation and builds the skill of focusing attention, which is beneficial both during meditation and in daily life.

Dealing with Challenges

It's common to face challenges such as restlessness, boredom, or an influx of thoughts during meditation. These are normal experiences and not indications of failure. The practice of meditation is essentially about returning your focus to the breath whenever you realize your mind has wandered. This might happen many times during a session, which is perfectly fine.

As you continue to practice, you will likely notice periods when your mind becomes calmer, and meditation feels more natural and effortless. However, each session might feel different, and it's important to approach each one with an open, non-judgmental attitude.

Expanding Your Practice

Once a basic practice of focusing on the breath has been established, you might explore other types of meditation, such as guided meditations, which can be found in books, apps, or online. Other practices might involve focusing on a mantra (a repeated word or phrase), doing a body scan (paying attention to various parts of the body), or practicing loving-kindness meditation (sending thoughts of love and well-being to yourself and others).

Meditation is a journey, not a destination. It's a personal and unique experience that can evolve over time, offering deeper insights into one's own mind and emotions. The key to successful meditation practice is consistency and patience. With regular practice, meditation can become a vital part of maintaining mental balance and overall well-being in your life.

ᐯᐯᐯ

"Mindfulness is not about being quiet; it's about becoming aware. It teaches us to live each moment as it unfolds, to recognize the richness of the present. In doing so, we carve a path to a more deliberate and considered life."

❦❦❦

FOUR
TYPES OF MEDITATION

Meditation is an umbrella term that encompasses a variety of techniques and practices aimed at promoting mental clarity, emotional calmness, and physical relaxation. Over thousands of years, different cultures around the world have developed their unique meditation practices, tailored to the needs and values of their societies. In modern times, this variety offers a rich palette from which individuals can choose a form that suits their lifestyle and objectives.

Mindfulness Meditation

Mindfulness meditation originates from Buddhist teachings and is one of the most widely practiced forms of meditation in the Western world. It involves paying attention to thoughts, sounds, the sensations of breathing, or parts of the body, bringing your focus back whenever the mind starts to wander. The goal is not to become involved with the thoughts or to judge them, but simply to be aware of each mental note as it arises.

This practice can be done sitting, standing, or walking, and is often the basis for other types of meditation. Mindfulness can be practiced at any time and anywhere, whether you're washing dishes, taking a shower, or walking to work, making it highly accessible and practical. The benefits of mindfulness meditation include reduced stress, improved concentration, increased emotional flexibility, and enhanced overall well-being.

Focused Attention Meditation

Focused attention meditation is highly effective in enhancing concentration. It involves focusing on a single point. This could be following the breath, repeating a single word or mantra, staring at a candle flame, listening to a repetitive sound, or counting beads on a mala. Because focusing the mind is challenging, a beginner might meditate for only a few minutes at a time, gradually increasing the duration as the ability to maintain focus improves.

The purpose of this form of meditation is to train the mind to focus voluntarily, without becoming distracted by external or internal stimuli. Regular practice improves attention and helps control the usual stream of thoughts that often invades our waking consciousness. This can be particularly helpful in reducing anxiety, which often arises from fear of future events or ruminations on the past.

Loving-Kindness Meditation

Also known as Metta meditation, loving-kindness meditation is the practice of directing well-wishes towards others and oneself. It typically involves opening the session by focusing on the breath or a visualisation, then progressing to the silent repetition of phrases that express goodwill, kindness, and compassion. Common phrases include "may you be happy," "may you be healthy," "may you be safe," and "may you live with ease."

Starting with oneself and gradually extending the circle of

compassion to include friends, acquaintances, and all living beings, this practice develops an attitude of love and kindness towards everything, even a person's enemies and sources of stress. Loving-kindness meditation is associated with increasing positivity, empathy, and compassionate behavior toward others.

Transcendental Meditation

Transcendental Meditation (TM) is a simple, silent form of meditation that requires sitting comfortably with one's eyes closed for 20 minutes twice a day. It involves the use of a mantra (a specific sound, word, or phrase) that is repeated in a specific way and is taught by a certified instructor. The practice is aimed at settling the mind to a state of "pure consciousness," where the meditator experiences a state of mental silence and profound relaxation without needing to use concentration or effort.

TM is known for its effectiveness on stress reduction and its ability to improve overall health and cognitive functions. Its simplicity and the fact that it does not require specific belief systems make it a popular choice among people of all ages and backgrounds.

Body Scan Meditation

Body scan meditation focuses on bodily sensations in a progressive sequence throughout the body. Starting from the toes and moving upwards, practitioners focus on the physical sensations in each part of their body, noticing any discomfort, tension, or warmth. This form of meditation is often used in mindfulness-based stress reduction (MBSR) programs and helps to cultivate a heightened awareness of the physical body. It can also serve as a relaxing practice before sleep.

Yoga and Meditation

While not a meditation technique in the traditional sense, yoga incorporates many meditative practices through controlled breathing and poses that encourage concentration and improved body awareness. Yoga practices vary widely, but most share the common goal of harmonizing body and mind, preparing both for deeper spiritual practices such as meditation.

The diversity in meditation practices provides a variety of pathways for individuals seeking mental clarity, emotional stability, physical relaxation, or a deeper spiritual connection. Each technique offers unique benefits and can be adapted to fit different personal preferences and lifestyle needs. Whether you are drawn to the simplicity of focused attention, the emotional enrichment of loving-kindness, or the structured approach of Transcendental Meditation, there is a meditation style that can enhance your life and lead to greater peace and fulfillment.

ᕉᕉᕉ

"In the garden of the mind, thoughts are the seeds
we plant. Meditation helps us cultivate patience and
care, allowing us to grow flowers where there once
were weeds. It's not about clearing the garden but
nurturing what serves us."

ᛒᛒᛒ

FIVE

MINDFULNESS IN DAILY LIFE

Mindfulness, a practice rooted in ancient meditation traditions, is now embraced worldwide for its ability to enhance mental clarity, emotional balance, and overall wellbeing. This simple yet profound practice involves being fully present and engaged with whatever we are doing at the moment, without distraction or judgment. Integrating mindfulness into daily life isn't about adding more activities to our schedule; rather, it's about changing our approach to our daily activities.

Starting the Day Mindfully

A mindful start sets the tone for the day. Before jumping out of bed, spend a few minutes in bed upon waking, breathing deeply and acknowledging your feelings, thoughts, and bodily sensations. This simple practice helps center your mind and prepare you for the day ahead. As you brush your teeth, take a shower, and eat breakfast, fully engage with these activities. Notice the taste of your food, the sensation of water on your skin, and the texture of the toothbrush. These moments of awareness can transform routine tasks into a series of peaceful experiences, reducing stress and enhancing appreciation for the mundane.

Mindful Commuting

Commuting can be a source of stress and autopilot behavior, but it also presents a perfect opportunity to practice mindfulness. If you drive, notice the grip of your hands on the steering wheel, the tension in your shoulders, and the scenery you pass by. If you use public transportation, take the time to observe your breath and the sounds around you. Instead of scrolling through your phone, try to be present with your surroundings. This can transform travel time into a meditative practice, allowing you to arrive at your destination more relaxed and aware.

Mindfulness at Work

The workplace is often a hub of stress and distraction, making it a crucial area for mindfulness practice. Start by organizing your workspace each morning, creating a clean and ordered environment that can help minimize stress. Throughout the day, take short breaks to practice deep breathing or to simply sit and observe your surroundings without judgment. During meetings, listen actively, focusing completely on the speaker instead of planning what you will say next. By being fully present, you can enhance your performance and improve your interactions with colleagues.

Mindful Eating

Mindful eating is about experiencing food more intensely and recognizing our body's hunger and fullness signals. Start by serving smaller portions and eating without distractions like TV or smartphones. Chew slowly, savoring each bite and paying attention to the textures and flavors of your food. This practice can help improve digestion and prevent overeating by making you more attuned to your body's needs and signals.

Mindfulness in Relationships

Being present with loved ones is perhaps one of the most important applications of mindfulness. It involves giving them your full attention during conversations, free from distractions like electronic devices. Listen deeply, without preparing your response while the other person is speaking. This level of engagement can significantly enhance your relationships, making your interactions more meaningful and fulfilling.

Mindful Leisure

Even during leisure activities, mindfulness can enhance enjoyment and relaxation. Whether reading a book, taking a walk, or engaging in hobbies, fully immerse yourself in these activities. Notice the details and sensations associated with each action. This focus not only increases enjoyment but also helps in developing a deeper connection to the activity.

Ending the Day Mindfully

Just as you start the day mindfully, ending it mindfully can promote better sleep and a sense of closure. Spend the last few minutes before bed reflecting on the day's events, acknowledging your feelings about them without judgment. Practice gratitude for the day's positive aspects and let go of any disappointments or stresses. A simple nighttime meditation or gentle yoga can also help calm the mind and prepare the body for sleep.

Challenges to Mindfulness

Despite its simplicity, integrating mindfulness into daily life can be challenging. Distractions, old habits, and the pace of modern life can easily pull us away from being present. It's helpful to remember that mindfulness is a practice, and like any skill, it improves with consistency and patience. When you notice you've become distracted, gently guide your attention back to the present moment without criticism.

Incorporating mindfulness into daily life transforms ordinary activities into moments of awareness, growth, and potential joy. By regularly practicing mindfulness, you can cultivate a state of mental clarity and emotional equilibrium that enhances every aspect of your life, making every day a richer, more vibrant experience.

ᐅᐅᐅ

"The strength of meditation lies in its simplicity. It asks only for presence, only for breathing, only for awareness. Yet, in these simple acts, we find worlds of peace and reservoirs of resilience."

ppp

SIX

OVERCOMING CHALLENGES IN MEDITATION

Meditation offers a plethora of benefits, from enhanced mental clarity to deeper peace of mind. However, beginners and seasoned practitioners alike can face challenges that might discourage them from continuing the practice. Some of the most common hurdles include restlessness, distractions, and a perceived lack of time.

Dealing with Restlessness

Restlessness during meditation is a common experience, especially for beginners whose minds are accustomed to constant activity. When trying to sit quietly, you may find that your legs itch to move, or your mind races without pause. The first step in overcoming this is to acknowledge restlessness as a natural response and not a failure on your part.

To cope with restlessness, it can be helpful to incorporate some physical activity, like a short walk or some light stretching, before settling down to meditate. This can help dispel some of the physical energy that contributes to restlessness.

Additionally, during meditation, it's important to adopt a comfortable posture. If sitting for long periods is challenging, consider using a meditation bench, a cushion, or even adopting a lying-down position as long as it doesn't encourage sleep.

Another technique is to turn the mind's restlessness into an object of meditation. Observe the feeling of restlessness without judgment or engagement. Ask yourself where the restlessness is felt in the body and describe the sensations associated with it. This can paradoxically help diminish the power of restlessness by increasing your awareness and acceptance of the present moment.

Managing Distractions

Distractions are inevitable in meditation, whether they come from external sources like noise or internal sources like wandering thoughts.

The key to dealing with distractions is not to try to eliminate them but to improve your reaction to them. When you notice a distraction, acknowledge it and gently bring your focus back to your meditation object, whether it's your breath, a mantra, or a visualization.

Creating a conducive environment can also minimize distractions. Try to meditate in a quiet space where interruptions are less likely. Informing others in your household of your meditation schedule can help ensure you are not disturbed. Additionally, using noise-canceling headphones or a white noise machine can help block external noise.

Finding Time to Meditate

One of the most common barriers to meditation is the feeling of not having enough time. Yet, the flexibility of meditation is that it doesn't require a lengthy commitment. Even five minutes can be beneficial, and short, consistent sessions are better than sporadic longer ones.

To incorporate meditation into your daily routine, link it to a habitual activity like brushing your teeth or having your morning coffee. This can help turn meditation into a habit. Setting a specific time for meditation, such as during lunch breaks or right before bed, can also help it become a part of your daily routine.

For those with extremely tight schedules, integrating mindfulness practices into daily activities can also be effective. This can include being fully present and attentive while eating, walking, or even during conversations. These practices do not require extra time out of your day but can still provide significant benefits.

Embracing Imperfection

Many beginners hold an idealized view of meditation as a state of profound peace and enlightenment, becoming frustrated when their experience doesn't match these expectations. It's vital to understand that meditation is a practice, and like all skills, it requires patience and persistence. The mind's tendency to wander is natural, and each return to focus is actually a moment of success, not failure.

Meditation is not about achieving perfection but about enhancing awareness and fostering a deeper understanding of oneself and one's environment.

Each session offers a unique experience, and challenges are part of the journey, providing opportunities for growth. By adopting practical strategies to deal with restlessness, distractions, and time constraints, you can maintain a consistent practice that grows more rewarding over time.

Embracing the obstacles as part of the learning process can turn them into valuable lessons that enrich your meditation experience. As you continue to practice, you'll find that meditation becomes less about doing something right and more about being present in the moment.

ᐅᐅᐅ

"To meditate is to converse with the inner self. It's a dialogue where words are silent but meaning profound. In this quiet space, we find answers that the noise of life often obscures."

ᐅᐅᐅ

SEVEN

DEEPENING YOUR PRACTICE

For many who start on the path of meditation, the initial challenges are about making it a regular part of life and coping with basic distractions. Once these hurdles are overcome and the basics of meditation are well understood, the next natural step is to deepen the practice. This phase of the meditation journey is about enhancing the quality of the experience, achieving greater insight, and reaching new levels of spiritual and emotional growth. Here are some techniques and suggestions to help deepen your meditation practice.

Extending the Duration

One of the simplest ways to deepen your meditation practice is to gradually increase the length of your sessions. If you are comfortable meditating for ten minutes, consider extending this time to fifteen or twenty minutes. Lengthening your meditation time allows you to explore a more profound state of stillness and silence, where deeper insights can occur. As you sit for longer periods, you learn to witness and let go of persistent thoughts and patterns that surface, providing a deeper understanding of your mind.

Exploring Different Meditation Techniques

While consistency in one type of meditation technique has its benefits, exploring various forms can enhance and deepen your understanding of meditation and yourself. If you have been practicing focused attention on the breath, for example, try incorporating mindfulness meditation, where you observe your thoughts without attachment. Alternatively, delve into loving-kindness meditation to cultivate feelings of compassion and love, which can add a rich emotional layer to your practice.

Experimenting with less familiar forms of meditation, such as Zazen, Vipassana, or transcendental meditation, can also provide fresh insights and bring renewed enthusiasm to your practice. Each style has unique nuances and benefits, challenging you in different ways and often leading to surprising personal discoveries.

Incorporating Retreats

Attending a meditation retreat is another effective way to deepen your practice. Retreats provide an opportunity to focus exclusively on meditation away from the distractions and responsibilities of everyday life. They often involve several days of intensive meditation practice under the guidance of experienced instructors, which can help you break through plateaus and gain new insights. The immersive experience of a retreat can significantly accelerate your understanding and appreciation of meditation.

Regularly Attending Group Sessions

While meditation is often practiced alone, joining a meditation group can add a valuable communal element to your practice. Meditating with others can not only be motivating but also deepen your practice through the shared energy and focus of the group.

Regular attendance at group sessions can also connect you with a community of like-minded individuals who can provide support, share experiences, and offer guidance.

Deepening Understanding Through Study

Complementing your practice with study can enrich your understanding and commitment. Reading texts on meditation, whether contemporary books or ancient scriptures, can provide philosophical insights and practical advice that enhance your practice. Additionally, listening to talks by seasoned practitioners can expose you to new ideas and perspectives, deepening your knowledge and inspiring your practice.

Mindfulness Throughout the Day

Integrating mindfulness into your daily activities can significantly enhance the depth of your meditation practice. By maintaining an attitude of mindfulness throughout the day—not just during formal meditation sessions—you cultivate a continuous state of awareness and presence. This constant practice can help you observe your mental habits and patterns more clearly and bring about profound transformations in your response to daily stresses and challenges.

Journaling Your Experiences

Keeping a meditation journal is a helpful tool for deepening your practice. After each session, take a few moments to jot down what you experienced, what thoughts emerged, how your body felt, and any emotions that arose. Over time, reviewing your journal can offer insights into your progress, patterns, and the subtle ways in which your practice is affecting your life. It can also serve as a reflective tool, helping you to understand deeper aspects of your mind and emotional landscape.

Deepening your meditation practice is a journey unique to each individual, filled with personal discoveries and challenges. By extending your practice time, exploring various meditation techniques, attending retreats, engaging with a community, studying meditation philosophies, integrating mindfulness into everyday life, and journaling your experiences, you can develop a richer, more profound meditation practice. These steps not only enhance your sessions but also bring the peace and insight gained during meditation into all aspects of your life, leading to a more mindful, compassionate, and introspective existence.

ᗡᗡᗡ

"Meditation is the delicate art of doing nothing
actively and letting go gracefully. It teaches us that
not all battles are won by action; some are won by
surrender. In surrender, we find the power to let go
and the clarity to move forward."

❦❦❦

EIGHT

MEDITATION AND EMOTIONAL BALANCE

Emotional balance is crucial for a fulfilling and healthy life. It enables us to handle life's ups and downs with grace and composure, maintaining our mental well-being. Meditation has been shown to be a powerful tool in achieving this balance, helping to manage emotions and foster emotional resilience.

Understanding Emotional Responses

Emotions are a fundamental part of human experience, but when they become overwhelming or are poorly managed, they can lead to stress, anxiety, and depression. Our emotional responses are shaped by a complex interplay of brain chemistry, personal history, and the current environment. Typically, emotional reactions are automatic and not within our immediate control. However, meditation teaches us to observe our emotions without getting caught up in them, which is a crucial step in managing them more effectively.

The Role of Meditation in Emotional Regulation

Meditation helps in emotional regulation in several ways. First, it enhances our "metacognitive awareness," which is our ability to observe our thoughts and feelings without identifying with them. When we meditate, we practice watching our thoughts come and go. This helps us realize that emotions are transient and do not define us. Over time, this perspective makes us less reactive in emotional situations, providing a space between feeling an emotion and acting on it.

Second, meditation can change the way our brain responds to stress and emotions. Neuroscientific research has shown that regular meditation increases the density of gray matter in areas of the brain involved in emotional regulation, such as the prefrontal cortex, while decreasing activity in the amygdala, the area responsible for fear and emotional reactions. These changes help us respond to stressors with more calmness and less panic.

Meditation Techniques for Emotional Healing

Several meditation techniques are particularly effective in promoting emotional balance:

Mindfulness Meditation: This involves observing present thoughts and emotions without judgment. Practicing mindfulness allows you to notice emotional triggers and habitual reactions that may go unnoticed. Over time, this awareness builds a greater understanding of emotional patterns and provides more choice in how to respond to them.

Focused Attention Meditation: This type of meditation helps train your concentration and calm your mind, reducing the overall tendency toward emotional reactivity. By focusing on a single point, such as the breath or a mantra, you learn to maintain calm and poise, even in stressful situations.

Loving-Kindness Meditation (Metta): This practice involves directing thoughts of compassion and love towards oneself and others. It can be particularly beneficial for those suffering from emotional distress, as it fosters positive emotions and decreases negative feelings like resentment and anger.

Building Emotional Resilience

Emotional resilience refers to the ability to bounce back from stressful or adverse situations. Meditation strengthens emotional resilience by enhancing self-awareness and compassion, improving the ability to navigate through emotional upheavals without losing balance. It equips individuals with the tools to accept their emotional state without overidentification, promoting quicker recovery from emotional setbacks.

Practical Benefits in Daily Life

The emotional stability gained through regular meditation practice can have profound effects on everyday life. It can improve relationships by reducing impulsive reactions and increasing empathetic communication. In the workplace, it can lead to better stress management and enhanced creativity, as a calm mind is more capable of thinking outside the box and solving problems effectively.

Moreover, meditation can help manage and reduce symptoms of various emotional disorders such as anxiety, depression, and PTSD. By fostering a state of relaxation and present-moment awareness, meditation helps alleviate the pervasive ruminations that often characterize these conditions.

Meditation offers valuable tools for achieving emotional balance and resilience. By regularly engaging in meditation practices, individuals can enhance their ability to regulate emotions, respond to stress more constructively, and enjoy improved overall mental health. The benefits extend beyond the individual, positively impacting relationships, work, and the broader community. Embracing meditation as a regular practice can transform your approach to life, leading to a more balanced, resilient, and fulfilling existence.

ppp

"Each moment of mindfulness counts, like drops in
the ocean, seemingly insignificant yet part of vast
depths. Over time, these moments can calm the
stormiest seas of our minds. Such is the
transformative power of persistent practice."

ᐅᐅᐅ

NINE

Stress Reduction Through Meditation: Cultivating Calm in a Chaotic World

In today's fast-paced world, stress has become an unavoidable part of life for many people. From the pressures of work and financial responsibilities to personal relationships and health concerns, stress can manifest in various forms and affect every aspect of our lives. However, amidst the chaos, there exists a powerful tool for managing stress and promoting well-being: meditation.

Understanding Stress and Its Effects

Before delving into the benefits of meditation for stress reduction, it's essential to understand what stress is and how it impacts our lives. Stress is the body's natural response to perceived threats or challenges, triggering a cascade of physiological and psychological reactions aimed at preparing us to cope with the situation. While short-term stress can be adaptive and even motivating, chronic stress can have detrimental effects on our physical health, mental well-being, and overall quality of life.

Chronic stress has been linked to a host of health problems, including high blood pressure, heart disease, weakened immune function, and increased risk of mental health disorders such as anxiety and depression. Additionally, stress can impair cognitive function, disrupt sleep patterns, and contribute to feelings of overwhelm, irritability, and burnout. Given these significant implications, finding effective strategies to manage and reduce stress is crucial for maintaining optimal health and well-being.

The Role of Meditation in Stress Reduction

Meditation has long been recognized as a potent tool for promoting relaxation, reducing stress, and cultivating a sense of inner peace. Rooted in ancient spiritual traditions and practices, meditation encompasses a wide range of techniques and approaches that share a common goal: to quiet the mind, calm the body, and foster a state of deep relaxation and awareness.

One of the key mechanisms through which meditation reduces stress is by eliciting the relaxation response—a physiological state characterized by decreased heart rate, blood pressure, and muscle tension, as well as enhanced immune function and overall feelings of well-being. By engaging in regular meditation practice, individuals can train their bodies and minds to activate the relaxation response more readily, counteracting the harmful effects of chronic stress and promoting a greater sense of calm and equilibrium.

Practical Techniques for Stress Reduction

There are many different forms of meditation, each with its unique techniques and benefits. However, most meditation practices share some common elements that can be particularly effective for reducing stress and anxiety. Here are some practical techniques that anyone can incorporate into their daily routine:

Focused Attention Meditation: This technique involves directing your attention to a single point of focus, such as your breath, a mantra, or a specific object. By anchoring your awareness in the present moment, focused attention meditation helps quiet the mind and reduce the tendency to ruminate on past regrets or future worries.

Mindfulness Meditation: Mindfulness meditation involves cultivating non-judgmental awareness of your thoughts, feelings, bodily sensations, and the surrounding environment. By observing these experiences with curiosity and acceptance, mindfulness meditation helps you develop a greater sense of clarity and perspective, reducing the impact of stressors and promoting emotional resilience.

Body Scan Meditation: In body scan meditation, you systematically bring your attention to different parts of your body, starting from your toes and moving upward to your head. As you scan each body part, you notice any sensations or tensions present without judgment, allowing them to release and dissolve. Body scan meditation promotes relaxation and helps alleviate physical tension, which is often a manifestation of stress.

Loving-Kindness Meditation: Also known as metta meditation, loving-kindness meditation involves cultivating feelings of love, compassion, and goodwill toward oneself and others. By intentionally generating positive emotions and sending them out into the world, loving-kindness meditation counteracts negative emotions like fear, anger, and resentment, fostering emotional balance and connection.

Visualization Meditation: Visualization meditation involves mentally picturing a peaceful scene or desired outcome, engaging your senses to create a vivid and immersive experience. By visualizing yourself in a calm and serene environment or achieving a goal, you can evoke feelings of relaxation, confidence, and empowerment, reducing stress and increasing feelings of positivity.

Incorporating Meditation into Your Daily Life

The beauty of meditation is its accessibility and adaptability—it can be practiced anytime, anywhere, and by anyone, regardless of age, background, or physical ability. To reap the benefits of meditation for stress reduction, it's essential to establish a regular practice and integrate meditation into your daily life. Here are some tips for incorporating meditation into your routine:

Set Aside Time: Carve out dedicated time each day for meditation, whether it's first thing in the morning, during a lunch break, or before bed. Consistency is key, so aim to practice meditation at the same time and place each day to establish a habit.

Start Small: If you're new to meditation, start with just a few minutes each day and gradually increase the duration as you become more comfortable. Even just five to ten minutes of meditation can have significant benefits for reducing stress and promoting relaxation.

Create a Sacred Space: Designate a quiet, comfortable space in your home where you can practice meditation without distractions. You might choose to decorate this space with candles, cushions, or other items that evoke a sense of peace and tranquility.

Use Guided Meditations: If you're unsure where to start or find it challenging to quiet your mind on your own, consider using guided meditation recordings or smartphone apps that provide audio guidance and instruction. These resources can be helpful for beginners and experienced practitioners alike.

Be Patient and Persistent: Like any skill, meditation takes time and practice to master. Be patient with yourself and avoid judging your meditation sessions as "good" or "bad." Instead, approach each session with an open mind and a willingness to learn from whatever arises.

The Benefits of Consistent Practice

As you commit to a regular meditation practice, you may begin to notice subtle but profound changes in how you respond to stress and adversity. Over time, meditation can help you cultivate greater resilience, emotional balance, and inner peace, allowing you to navigate life's challenges with grace and equanimity. By incorporating meditation into your daily routine, you empower yourself to take control of your mental and emotional well-being, finding solace and strength in the midst of life's ups and downs.

Stress reduction through meditation is not just a theoretical concept but a practical and accessible tool that anyone can use to improve their quality of life. By learning to quiet the mind, cultivate awareness, and foster a sense of inner calm, you can effectively manage stress and anxiety, promote emotional resilience, and experience greater well-being and vitality. Whether you're seeking relief from chronic stress or simply looking to enhance your overall quality of life, meditation offers a path to greater peace, clarity, and fulfillment.

ᐅᐅᐅ

"*Meditation is the telescope through which we gaze into the cosmos of our soul. It shows us that the universe within is as vast and complex as the one above. And in this exploration, we find our place among the stars.*"

❦❦❦

TEN
MEDITATION AND RELATIONSHIPS

Building and maintaining healthy relationships are central to our overall happiness and well-being. The quality of our interactions with others—whether with family, friends, or colleagues—significantly affects our daily lives. Meditation, often viewed primarily as a tool for individual self-improvement, also offers profound benefits in the realm of interpersonal relationships. By fostering greater empathy, improving communication, and reducing reactivity, meditation can enhance the way we connect with others. This chapter explores how the practice of meditation can positively influence our relationships.

Fostering Empathy Through Meditation

Empathy is the ability to understand and share the feelings of another person, and it is a cornerstone of successful relationships. Meditation cultivates empathy by increasing our ability to regulate our emotions and heighten our awareness of others' feelings. Mindfulness meditation, for instance, enhances our ability to be present with another person without judgment. This presence allows us to perceive more deeply what others are experiencing and respond with genuine understanding.

Practices like loving-kindness meditation (Metta) specifically aim to develop feelings of compassion and goodwill towards others, including those we may find challenging. By regularly sending thoughts of love and kindness to friends, neutral individuals, and even our adversaries, we can break down barriers of resentment and improve our capacity for empathy.

Improving Communication Skills

Effective communication is vital in relationships, and meditation supports this in several ways. First, meditation can help us become better listeners. The practice of focusing on the present moment allows us to engage more fully when someone is speaking to us, rather than planning our next response or getting distracted by our thoughts and feelings. This attentiveness can make our interactions more meaningful and supportive.

Moreover, meditation helps in managing our speech. It fosters a greater awareness of our thoughts and emotions, allowing us to choose more carefully the words we use. With regular practice, we can learn to avoid reactive and hurtful comments and instead express ourselves more clearly and kindly. This mindful communication can prevent misunderstandings and conflicts and promote more harmonious relationships.

Reducing Reactivity

One of the significant challenges in relationships is emotional reactivity—responding impulsively to thoughts and emotions without considering the consequences. Meditation helps reduce this reactivity. By observing our mind in meditation, we learn to recognize our habitual emotional triggers and the patterns of reaction that typically follow. Over time, this awareness enables us to pause when triggered, choose how to respond, and thus avoid knee-jerk reactions that can damage relationships.

For instance, if a conversation with a partner or a colleague is becoming heated, a meditator can notice their rising anger or frustration and choose to take a few deep breaths to restore calm. This pause can make the difference between escalating a conflict and resolving it constructively.

Deepening Connections

Meditation can also deepen our connections with others by making us more attuned to the non-verbal elements of communication, such as body language and facial expressions. Mindfulness enhances our ability to perceive and interpret these subtle cues, which are often more telling than words. This heightened awareness can lead to more intimate and rewarding interactions, as we respond more sensitively to others' unspoken needs and emotions.

Practical Tips for Integrating Meditation into Relationships

Shared meditation: Practicing meditation together with a partner or family members can strengthen bonds and create a shared experience of calm and focus.

Mindful listening: Make a conscious effort to listen mindfully in conversations, giving full attention to the other person without interruption.

Regular reflection: After interactions, especially difficult ones, reflect on your role and how you might improve future communications using insights gained during meditation.

Compassion in action: Use insights from loving-kindness meditation to perform small acts of kindness for those around you, strengthening relationships and building positive feelings.

Incorporating meditation into daily life can significantly enhance interpersonal relationships. The practice develops empathy, improves communication, and reduces emotional reactivity, all of which contribute to healthier, more supportive, and more enjoyable relationships. By applying the principles of mindfulness and meditation, we can transform our interactions with others, promoting not only our happiness but also the well-being of those around us. Through meditation, we learn not only to live more harmoniously within ourselves but also with others, creating a more compassionate and connected world.

❧❧❧

"In the silence of meditation, we hear the whispers
of our true selves. These whispers, though soft,
carry the compelling truths of our existence.
Listening deeply, we align our actions with our
deepest values."

ᗺᗺᗺ

ELEVEN

Mindful Eating and Health

In today's fast-paced world, meals are often consumed quickly and without much thought. Amid the rush, the act of eating can become automatic or even a side activity done while multitasking. However, the way we eat can significantly affect our physical health and overall well-being. Mindful eating, a practice derived from the broader concept of mindfulness, involves paying full attention to the experience of eating and drinking, both inside and outside the body.

What is Mindful Eating?

Mindful eating is about using mindfulness to reach a state of full attention to your experiences, cravings, and physical cues when eating. Fundamentally, it involves eating slowly without distraction, noticing the colors, smells, textures, and flavors of the food, and being aware of the emotional and physical responses to eating. This practice can help shift eating behaviors, leading to improved digestion, a better relationship with food, and enhanced health.

Benefits of Mindful Eating

Improved Digestion: By eating slowly and chewing thoroughly, you give your digestive system enough time to process food efficiently, which can help in reducing digestive discomfort and improving nutrient absorption.

Enhanced Enjoyment: Slowing down and savoring each bite can help you appreciate the flavors and textures of your food, making meals more enjoyable and satisfying.

Weight Management: Mindful eating helps in recognizing when you are full, which prevents overeating—a common cause of weight gain. Being aware of hunger and fullness signals leads to more thoughtful eating behaviors, which can help in maintaining a healthy weight.

Reduced Emotional Eating: By recognizing the emotional reasons for eating, such as stress, boredom, or loneliness, you can develop healthier ways to cope with emotions, which may decrease unnecessary snacking or binge eating.

Developing a Healthier Relationship with Food: Mindful eating discourages labeling foods as "good" or "bad" and instead promotes a balanced view of nutrition. This can help reduce anxiety around eating and encourage a more peaceful relationship with food.

Practical Tips for Practicing Mindful Eating

Start with a Small Meal: Begin your practice with a small meal or snack. It's easier to pay attention to the experience of eating when the meal is not overwhelming.

Eliminate Distractions: Turn off the TV, put away your phone, and clear away books or other distractions from your eating area. This helps you focus on the meal and on your body's cues.

Engage All Senses: Before you begin eating, take a moment to appreciate the appearance and aroma of your food. As you eat, try to identify all the ingredients, including subtle herbs and spices.

Eat Slowly: Put down your utensils between bites, chew thoroughly, and savor each mouthful. This not only helps with digestion but also makes it easier to detect your body's fullness signals.

Check in with Your Body: Regularly assess your hunger and fullness levels during meals. Ask yourself whether you are eating out of hunger or habit. This can help you decide when to stop eating.

Consider the Impact of Your Food Choices: Think about where your food comes from and the nutritional benefits it offers. This can foster a deeper appreciation for your meals and help you make healthier choices.

Reflect on Your Eating: After finishing your meal, take a few moments to think about your experience. What did you like? What didn't you like? How do you feel physically and emotionally?

Integrating Mindful Eating into Your Lifestyle

Integrating mindful eating into your daily life doesn't have to be a daunting task. Start by choosing one meal per day to eat mindfully, or begin with just the first few bites of any meal. Over time, as the practice becomes more familiar, expand these mindful moments.

Mindful eating is a powerful tool for enhancing our physical health and emotional well-being. It allows us to truly experience and enjoy our food, improves our dietary habits, and can transform our relationship with food.

By bringing mindfulness to our meals, we not only nourish our bodies but also our minds, cultivating a practice that enriches our lives in every bite.

ᝐᝐᝐ

"Mindfulness brings a high resolution to the picture of our daily life. It sharpens the image so we can see what's truly there, not just what we imagine or fear. Such clarity transforms both perception and reality."

❤❤❤

TWELVE

MEDITATION FOR DIFFERENT AGE GROUPS

Meditation is a versatile practice that can be adapted to benefit individuals at any stage of life. From young children to the elderly, each age group can find in meditation a tool for enhancing well-being, managing stress, and improving overall health.

Meditation for Children

Introducing meditation to children can provide them with early tools for stress management, focus, and emotional regulation. For young children, meditation should be simple and engaging. Techniques like guided imagery, where they imagine a quiet place like a beach or a forest, can be particularly effective. Additionally, breathing exercises using fun metaphors (e.g., "breathe in like you are smelling a flower, breathe out like you are blowing out a candle") can make the practice more accessible.

Sessions should be short to match children's shorter attention spans—typically a few minutes is sufficient. Regular practice can help improve children's attention, decrease anxiety, and enhance their emotional and social development. Integrating meditation into routine activities, such as a calming breath before starting schoolwork or a few moments of quiet before bedtime, can help make meditation a natural part of their daily life.

Meditation for Teenagers

Teenagers often face significant stress from academic pressures, social dynamics, and the challenges of transitioning into adulthood. Meditation can be a valuable resource for them, helping to manage anxiety, boost self-esteem, and improve concentration. Techniques such as mindfulness meditation are particularly suitable, as they teach teens to focus on the present moment and develop a non-judgmental awareness of their thoughts and feelings.

For teenagers, relating meditation to their interests or incorporating it into physical activities, such as yoga or martial arts, can increase its appeal. Also, using apps designed for meditation can resonate well with tech-savvy teens, providing guided sessions that they can follow on their own. Encouraging teens to meditate for a few minutes each day can help them develop a routine that strengthens their mental health and emotional resilience.

Meditation for Adults

Adults often turn to meditation to relieve stress, improve health, and find a deeper sense of purpose. For adults, the focus may be on techniques that can be integrated into a busy lifestyle, such as mindfulness, which can be practiced while commuting, eating, or taking a break at work. Deep breathing exercises, progressive muscle relaxation, and body scan meditations are also beneficial, helping to reduce stress and enhance body awareness.

Adults may benefit from longer meditation sessions than children and teenagers, ranging from 10 to 30 minutes or more. Establishing a regular practice before or after work, or during lunch breaks, can provide a structured way to relieve stress and increase productivity and creativity.

Meditation for the Elderly

For the elderly, meditation can help manage chronic pain, improve sleep patterns, and enhance overall mental health. It can also offer a sense of calm and connectedness in a phase of life that may involve significant changes, such as retirement or dealing with health issues. Techniques such as loving-kindness meditation can be particularly uplifting, fostering feelings of compassion towards oneself and others.

Elderly individuals might appreciate forms of meditation that incorporate gentle movement, such as tai chi or qigong, which are soft martial arts forms that combine meditation, controlled breathing, and gentle movement to enhance health and balance. These practices not only provide the meditative benefits but also help in maintaining physical health and mobility.

Meditation is a flexible practice that can be adapted to suit the needs of any age group. Whether through engaging visualizations for children, mindfulness for teenagers and adults, or gentle movement-based practices for the elderly, meditation offers significant benefits across the lifespan. By tailoring practices to be age-appropriate and relevant, meditation can provide powerful tools for enhancing well-being and coping with the varied challenges of different life stages. Through regular practice, individuals can experience improvements in their mental, emotional, and physical health, contributing to a richer, more balanced life.

ppp

"Meditation does not remove us from the world but draws us deeper into it. It is through this deep immersion that we see the interconnectedness of all things. And with this understanding, compassion flows naturally."

ᗵᗵᗵ

THIRTEEN

MEDITATION AND SLEEP

Sleep is a crucial component of overall health, impacting everything from cognitive performance to immune function. However, many people struggle with insomnia or poor sleep quality due to stress, anxiety, or other factors. Meditation has been shown to be an effective tool for enhancing sleep, helping individuals relax, fall asleep faster, and enjoy more restorative sleep.

Understanding the Connection Between Meditation and Sleep

Meditation helps improve sleep by addressing some of the common root causes of insomnia, including stress and anxiety. By calming the mind and reducing the fight-or-flight response of the nervous system, meditation can lower stress hormone levels and create conditions conducive to sleep. Regular meditation practice not only helps in falling asleep quicker but also deepens the quality of sleep, making it more refreshing.

Techniques for Improving Sleep Through Meditation

Mindfulness Meditation: Mindfulness involves paying attention to the present moment without judgment. Practicing mindfulness meditation at bedtime can help clear the mind of the day's stresses and focus on the rhythm of your breath, facilitating a peaceful transition to sleep. You can begin by observing the breath, noticing the cool air entering your nostrils and the warm air exiting, or by conducting a body scan starting from your toes to your head, releasing tension in each body part as you go.

Guided Imagery: This technique involves visualizing a peaceful setting and immersing yourself in its details. This distraction from usual thoughts helps the body relax. Listening to guided imagery through an app or audio recording can be particularly effective in shifting your focus from worries that interfere with sleep.

Mantra Meditation: Repeating a calming word or phrase, such as "peace" or "relax," can help focus the mind and ease into sleep. The repetitive nature of a mantra can act as a mental lullaby, reducing the brain's activity and facilitating sleep.

Breathing Exercises: Specific breathing techniques can also promote relaxation and sleep. The "4-7-8" breathing technique, where you breathe in for four seconds, hold the breath for seven seconds, and exhale for eight seconds, is especially effective. This pattern can reduce anxiety and help the body transition to sleep.

Progressive Muscle Relaxation (PMR): PMR involves tensing each muscle group in the body tightly, but not to the point of strain, and then slowly relaxing them. This helps highlight the contrast between tension and relaxation, guiding the body deeper into a state of calm. Starting from the toes and moving upwards can systematically relax the entire body, preparing it for sleep.

Incorporating Meditation into Your Nightly Routine

To effectively use meditation as a sleep aid, incorporate it into your nightly routine. This regularity helps the body and mind associate the meditation practice with the onset of sleep, reinforcing the habit. Here are some tips to integrate meditation into your nightly schedule:

Set a specific time: Meditate at the same time each night to strengthen the sleep association.

Create a conducive environment: Ensure your meditation space is comfortable, quiet, and free from distractions. You might include comfortable pillows, dim lighting, or calming scents like lavender.

Limit screen time: Reduce exposure to screens and bright lights at least an hour before bed to enhance the effectiveness of your meditation practice.

Keep it short: Start with 10-15 minutes of meditation. A longer session might be too stimulating before bed for some people.

Dealing with Common Challenges

It's common to face challenges when first using meditation to improve sleep. You may find your mind wandering back to the stressors of the day or becoming frustrated if sleep doesn't come immediately. It's important to approach these challenges with a mindset of patience and non-judgment.

The goal of meditation is not to force sleep but to create a relaxed state that is conducive to sleep. With regular practice, meditation can significantly enhance both the ease of falling asleep and the quality of sleep itself.

Incorporating meditation into your nightly routine can transform your sleep experience. With practices ranging from mindfulness to guided imagery, breathing exercises, and progressive muscle relaxation, you can find the technique that best suits your needs.

As you continue to practice, you may find not only improved sleep but also reduced stress and enhanced overall well-being, contributing to a healthier, more balanced life.

❦❦❦

"Through meditation, we learn that stillness is not the absence of movement but the correct alignment of our mind, body, and spirit. Here, in the equilibrium of existence, we find a peace that endures beyond time."

ppp

FOURTEEN

INTEGRATING MEDITATION INTO YOUR WORK LIFE

In today's fast-paced and often high-pressure work environments, stress is a common affliction that can hinder productivity and overall job satisfaction. However, integrating meditation into your work life offers a practical and effective method to not only reduce stress but also enhance focus, efficiency, and creativity. Here we will learn how mindfulness and meditation can be seamlessly incorporated into the workplace, offering strategies for individuals at all levels to foster a healthier, more balanced, and productive work environment.

Understanding the Benefits of Meditation in the Workplace

The practice of meditation, particularly mindfulness, has been shown to provide numerous benefits in the context of work. These include improved concentration and attention, enhanced ability to manage stress and react more calmly in challenging situations, better decision-making skills, and increased resilience against psychological stress. Additionally, mindfulness can promote emotional intelligence, leading to better interpersonal relations and enhanced teamwork skills.

Simple Techniques to Incorporate Meditation at Work

Mindful Breathing: This is one of the simplest and most effective ways to center yourself and combat stress. You can practice mindful breathing at your desk or during a break. Spend just a few minutes focusing on your breath, noticing each inhale and exhale, and returning your focus to your breathing whenever your mind wanders. This practice can serve as a mental reset, clearing your mind and reducing stress.

Scheduled Meditation Breaks: Just as you might take a coffee break, you can schedule short meditation breaks throughout your day. These can be formal sitting meditations, using an app or audio guide, or simply spending a few minutes in silence. Regularly stepping away from work tasks to meditate can help maintain steady productivity throughout the day and prevent burnout.

Mindful Listening: During meetings or conversations, practice fully focusing on the speaker, setting aside your own thoughts and distractions. This not only improves your ability to absorb information and respond thoughtfully but also enhances your interpersonal relationships by making colleagues feel heard and valued.

Mindful Eating: Use your lunch break to practice mindful eating. Instead of working or scrolling through your phone while you eat, focus solely on the experience of eating. Pay attention to the taste, texture, and aroma of your food. Eating mindfully helps improve digestion and can make your breaks more refreshing.

Walking Meditations: If your job involves sitting for long periods, incorporate short walking meditations into your day. Take a five to ten-minute walk, indoors or outside, and use this time to focus on your movement and breath. This not only helps stretch your legs and clear your mind but also integrates a meditative practice into your physical activity.

Creating a Mindful Work Environment

In addition to individual practices, fostering a workplace culture that values and understands the benefits of meditation can multiply its positive effects. Here are some strategies to encourage a more mindful workplace:

Educate and Encourage: Share resources about the benefits of meditation with your team or leadership. Proposing regular meditation sessions or mindfulness training can help cultivate a more focused and less stressful work environment.

Set Up a Quiet Space: If possible, set up a quiet room where employees can go to meditate or just sit quietly away from their desks. Having a physical space dedicated to relaxation and mindfulness can significantly enhance the feasibility of integrating meditation into the workday.

Lead by Example: If you are in a leadership position, practicing mindfulness openly can set a powerful example for your team. Leaders who demonstrate stress management and mindfulness in their behavior encourage their employees to adopt similar practices.

Dealing with Challenges

Integrating meditation into your work life may initially be met with skepticism or resistance, both from yourself and others. It's important to start small and gradually increase the visibility and acceptance of meditation practices. Highlighting the personal and organizational benefits through workshops or informational sessions can also help in gaining wider acceptance.

Integrating meditation into work life is not just about reducing stress or enhancing personal productivity; it's also about creating a healthier, more mindful workplace where employees can thrive. By adopting simple meditation techniques and fostering a supportive environment, companies and individuals alike can experience significant improvements in performance, satisfaction, and overall workplace well-being. These practices not only benefit individual employees but also contribute to a more positive, productive, and harmonious organizational culture.

"Meditation teaches us the art of metacognition—to think about thinking. This self-awareness is the first step toward intellectual freedom and emotional intelligence. By observing our thoughts, we choose which ones to engage with.

ᐅᐅᐅ

FIFTEEN

MEDITATION RETREATS AND COMMUNITY

Meditation is often seen as a solitary activity, something individuals do alone, in a quiet place, away from the hustle and bustle of everyday life. However, meditation can also be a communal practice, one that is enriched and deepened through shared experiences and mutual support. Meditation retreats and community groups offer unique environments where individuals can explore meditation more deeply, learn from others, and build a support network that enhances their practice.

The Power of Meditation Retreats

Meditation retreats are intensive meditation sessions, which can last from a weekend to several weeks. These retreats offer a structured opportunity to deepen one's practice away from the daily distractions and responsibilities of regular life. One of the primary benefits of attending a retreat is the chance to immerse oneself fully in meditation, often under the guidance of experienced instructors. This immersion can lead to profound experiences and breakthroughs in personal practice that might not occur in the usual, more fragmented daily sessions.

Deepening Practice in a Supported Environment

Retreats provide a supportive environment where every aspect of the day is designed to reinforce mindfulness and concentration. The daily schedule usually includes multiple meditation sessions, teachings on meditation principles, group discussions, and sometimes periods of silence that help deepen self-awareness and mindfulness. Being in a setting where others are similarly engaged helps participants stay motivated and gain insights from the collective experience.

Community as a Source of Learning and Connection

Another significant aspect of meditation retreats is the sense of community they foster. Being surrounded by like-minded individuals focused on similar goals can create a strong sense of belonging and shared purpose. For many, these connections become a source of friendship and support that lasts beyond the retreat, helping sustain the motivation for regular practice.

Benefits of Joining Meditation Groups

Apart from retreats, regular participation in local meditation groups or communities can also enhance one's practice. Meditation groups typically meet regularly, providing a structured time and space for communal meditation that can help maintain consistency in one's practice.

Consistency and Accountability

Meeting regularly with a group can create a sense of accountability, encouraging members to stick with their meditation practice, particularly on days when motivation might be low. Regular sessions also allow for the establishment of a routine, which is a crucial aspect of deepening meditation practice.

Shared Experiences and Emotional Support

Group settings provide an opportunity to share experiences, challenges, and successes related to meditation. This sharing can be incredibly validating, particularly for those who are new to meditation or who find certain aspects of the practice challenging. Knowing others are experiencing similar hurdles or breakthroughs can provide comfort and insights into overcoming personal obstacles.

Access to Guidance and Diverse Perspectives

Meditation groups often have experienced practitioners or teachers who can offer guidance and answer questions. This access to experienced insight can accelerate learning and help clarify confusions about the practice. Additionally, being part of a diverse group allows individuals to hear different perspectives and approaches to meditation, enriching their understanding and potentially introducing them to new techniques.

Integrating Community into Personal Practice

To effectively integrate the benefits of community into personal meditation practice, consider the following steps:

Regular Attendance: Commit to attending group sessions or retreats regularly. This commitment will help you build a routine and deepen your practice through continuous learning.

Engagement: Actively participate in discussions and activities. Engagement not only enhances your learning but also contributes to the community, making it a richer resource for others.

Mindfulness in Interactions: Practice mindfulness during interactions with community members. This practice can extend the benefits of meditation into your social skills, improving how you communicate and empathize with others.

Volunteer: If possible, volunteer within these communities. Helping to organize meetings or events can deepen your connection to the group and enhance your sense of purpose and belonging.

Meditation retreats and communities offer valuable opportunities to deepen one's practice and connect with others who share a commitment to mindfulness. Whether through intensive retreats or regular local group meetings, these communal practices can significantly enhance the benefits of meditation, providing support, accountability, and a deeper sense of connection both to the practice and to others. By embracing the communal aspects of meditation, practitioners can enrich their experience and sustain their practice over time, fostering both personal growth and community well-being.

ϷϷϷ

"In the dance of life, mindfulness is our rhythm keeper. It allows us to move gracefully between tasks, ensuring our steps are deliberate and our presence full. This rhythm is not hurried but harmoniously aligned with our breath."

ᎧᎧᎧ

SIXTEEN
USING TECHNOLOGY TO AID MEDITATION

In today's digital age, technology often gets a bad rap for being a distraction, but when used mindfully, it can be a powerful ally in enhancing personal growth and wellness practices such as meditation. A variety of technological tools, including apps and online resources, have been developed to support and deepen meditation practice. These tools make meditation more accessible, provide structured guidance, and help integrate the practice into daily life for people from all walks of life.

The Role of Meditation Apps

Meditation apps are perhaps the most significant technological advancement in supporting personal meditation practice. These apps are designed to make meditation accessible to everyone, regardless of their experience level or lifestyle. They offer a range of guided meditations, instructional videos, and customizable sessions to fit various needs and preferences. Here are some of the key features and benefits of using meditation apps:

Guided Meditations: Many users find it easier to meditate with a guide, especially in the beginning. Meditation apps typically offer a wide array of guided sessions from various traditions, led by experienced instructors. These guides can help users through the process, from how to sit to what to think about, or not think about.

Tracking Progress: Apps often include features that track progress, such as the number of consecutive days you've meditated, the total time spent meditating, and other mindfulness activities. This data can motivate users to stick with their meditation routine and can be rewarding to look back on.

Accessibility and Convenience: With a smartphone, users can meditate anytime and anywhere. Whether it's during a lunch break at work, on a morning commute, or before bed, meditation apps make it easy to engage in practice at convenient times.

Variety of Techniques: Apps offer various meditation techniques, including mindfulness, progressive relaxation, loving-kindness, and body scans, allowing users to explore different types of meditation and find what works best for them.

Community Features: Some apps also include community features where users can join challenges, share progress with friends, or participate in group meditations, adding a social element to the practice.

Popular Meditation Apps

Several meditation apps have gained popularity for their quality, user-friendliness, and the depth of resources offered. Apps like Headspace and Calm are well-known for their comprehensive meditation libraries, which cater to a range of goals, from reducing stress to improving sleep. Insight Timer features thousands of free meditations and is noted for its large, global community of users and teachers. Each app has its unique strengths, so users might try a few different ones to see which aligns best with their needs and preferences.

Online Meditation Resources

Beyond apps, the internet is full of resources that can support meditation practice. Many websites offer free access to meditation advice, articles, tutorials, and guided sessions. YouTube, for example, has countless meditation channels with sessions led by experienced practitioners. These resources are invaluable for those who wish to deepen their understanding of different meditation techniques or find inspiration for their practice.

Online Courses: Websites like Coursera and Udemy offer courses on meditation and mindfulness. These courses often include video lectures, readings, and exercises that provide a structured and comprehensive learning experience.

Podcasts: Numerous podcasts are dedicated to meditation and mindfulness, offering lessons, guided practices, and discussions on the benefits of meditation. Podcasts are an excellent option for those who prefer auditory learning or like to incorporate meditation into their daily walks or commutes.

Virtual Retreats: Some platforms provide virtual retreat experiences, which can be a great alternative for those who cannot attend a retreat in person due to time or budget constraints.

Integrating Technology Mindfully

While technology can greatly enhance meditation practice, it's important to use it mindfully. Dependence on digital devices can sometimes lead to distraction or a disconnection from the present moment. It's beneficial to maintain a balance—using these tools to support, rather than dominate, your meditation practice. Setting boundaries, such as turning off non-essential notifications during meditation, can help maintain this balance.

Technology, when used intentionally and mindfully, can be a valuable ally in developing and sustaining a meditation practice. Meditation apps and online resources make learning and practicing meditation more accessible and flexible, offering a range of tools that can be tailored to individual needs. By wisely integrating these technological tools, individuals can enhance their practice and experience the profound benefits of meditation more consistently in their daily lives.

❧❧❧

"Every mindful breath anchors us in the present,
detaching us from the tangles of the past and the
anxieties for the future. In this anchorage, we find
the freedom to live fully, to love deeply, and to
embrace the now."

ᐅᐅᐅ

SEVENTEEN

YOGA AND MEDITATION: PATHWAYS TO HOLISTIC WELLNESS

Yoga and meditation are ancient practices that have been linked for thousands of years, sharing a deep spiritual lineage. Both are powerful methods for improving physical health and enhancing mental clarity, but together, they offer a comprehensive approach to holistic wellness.

Understanding Yoga and Meditation

Yoga, much like meditation, originated in ancient India. It includes physical postures (asanas), breath control (pranayama), and meditation practices that are designed to unify the body, mind, and spirit. While many in the Western world associate yoga primarily with its physical aspects, the ultimate goal of traditional yoga is much deeper. It aims to prepare the body for prolonged meditation and to achieve a state of spiritual enlightenment.

Meditation, on the other hand, is the practice of focusing the mind and achieving mental clarity and emotional calm through various techniques, including mindfulness, concentration, and visualization. While meditation can be practiced independently of physical activity, integrating it with yoga provides a holistic approach that enhances both physical and mental well-being.

The Complementary Nature of Yoga and Meditation

Yoga and meditation complement each other in multiple ways. Practicing yoga can prepare the body for meditation by releasing tension, improving flexibility, and stabilizing energy levels. The physical practices of yoga promote endurance and strength, which can help individuals sit in meditation with greater ease and comfort for longer periods. Moreover, yoga's breathing exercises can directly influence the mind, settling restless thoughts and fostering a natural state of mental calm.

Conversely, meditation deepens the spiritual benefits of yoga by enhancing self-awareness and mindfulness. Through meditation, individuals can develop greater insight into their thoughts and emotions, which can lead to profound inner peace and emotional stability. This mental discipline also enhances the benefits of yoga by increasing the practitioner's awareness of their body, breath, and alignment during yoga poses, thus improving the overall efficacy and safety of the physical practice.

Practical Integration of Yoga and Meditation

Integrating yoga and meditation into daily life doesn't require extensive hours or an esoteric understanding of their philosophies. Here are some practical ways to incorporate both practices into everyday routines for holistic health:

Start with Gentle Yoga: Begin with simple yoga stretches that focus on breath and alignment. Early morning is an ideal time for yoga as it helps to invigorate the body and set a mindful tone for the day. Yoga practices such as Sun Salutations can be particularly energizing and can seamlessly transition into a meditation practice.

Incorporate Breathing Exercises: Pranayama, or yogic breathing, is a bridge between the physical practice of yoga and sitting meditation. Techniques like alternate nostril breathing or belly breathing can help regulate the energy flow in the body, calming the mind and preparing it for meditation.

Transition to Meditation: After a yoga session, the mind is typically more tranquil and the body more relaxed. This state is conducive for meditation. Post-yoga, try sitting in a comfortable position and meditate for a duration that feels appropriate, starting with just a few minutes and gradually increasing over time.

Daily Mindfulness: Throughout the day, maintain an attitude of mindfulness, which is a form of meditation. This can include being fully present while eating, working, or even during conversation. Such mindfulness practices can enhance the sense of calm and focus gained from yoga and meditation.

Regular Practice: Consistency is key in yoga and meditation. Aim to establish a routine that includes both practices, making them a regular part of your daily schedule. Over time, this regular practice will enhance your physical flexibility and mental clarity, contributing to an overall sense of well-being.

The Holistic Benefits

The combined practice of yoga and meditation offers extensive benefits. Physically, it promotes better posture, flexibility, and strength. Mentally, it enhances concentration, soothes stress, and can improve mood. Emotionally, the practices encourage self-acceptance and a greater sense of peace. Together, they provide a comprehensive toolkit for managing health in a holistic way, promoting harmony in the body, peace in the mind, and joy in the heart.

Yoga and meditation are more than just practices for physical and mental health; they are transformative tools that can enrich every aspect of life. By integrating these practices, individuals can achieve a greater balance and harmony between the body and the mind, paving the way for a healthier, more mindful, and spiritually connected life. Whether you are seeking physical health, mental clarity, or emotional stability, the synergy between yoga and meditation offers a proven path to holistic wellness.

ᗧᗧᗧ

"*Meditation is the subtle force that quiets the chaos within. It does not fight the noise but soothes it into silence, transforming the cacophony of our fears and desires into a symphony of peace and clarity.*"

ʕʕʕ

EIGHTEEN

Mindful Movement Practices

While meditation is often associated with stillness and seated postures, incorporating movement can enhance and diversify the practice, making it more accessible and enjoyable for many people. Mindful movement practices such as walking meditation, tai chi, and gentle yoga combine the physical benefits of movement with the mental and emotional benefits of meditation.

Understanding Mindful Movement

Mindful movement involves performing physical activity with intentional awareness, focusing on the sensations of the body and the breath, and cultivating a meditative state of mind. This form of practice is particularly beneficial for those who find it difficult to sit still for traditional meditation sessions or those who seek to incorporate mindfulness into a more active lifestyle.

Types of Mindful Movement Practices

Walking Meditation: Unlike casual walking, walking meditation involves intentionally noticing each step and the sensations in the body as you move. It can be practiced anywhere—whether in a quiet forest, a park, or even a busy city sidewalk. The key is to walk slowly and with deliberate awareness, synchronizing the movement with your breath, and noticing the lift and fall of each foot, the swing of your arms, and the feel of the ground under your feet.

Tai Chi: Often described as "meditation in motion," tai chi is a traditional Chinese martial art that emphasizes slow, graceful movements and deep, slow breathing. Each posture flows into the next without pause, keeping the body in constant motion. Tai chi helps reduce stress, improve balance and flexibility, and increase overall vitality and mental focus.

Gentle Yoga: Gentle yoga styles, such as Hatha or Yin Yoga, focus on slow movements, deep stretching, and mindful breathing. These practices allow for an exploration of the physical positions at a relaxed pace, promoting a meditative state through focused attention on the body and breath.

Benefits of Mindful Movement

Incorporating movement into meditation provides several benefits:

Enhances Physical Health: Mindful movement practices improve flexibility, balance, and strength. They also promote cardiovascular health, aid in muscle relaxation, and can help alleviate physical pain associated with sedentary lifestyles.

Reduces Mental Stress: Just like traditional meditation, mindful movement helps calm the mind and reduce stress. The physical activity involved also stimulates the release of endorphins, the body's natural mood elevators, which can create feelings of wellbeing and reduce the perception of pain.

Improves Focus and Mindfulness: These practices help sharpen mental focus and heighten bodily awareness. By concentrating on the movements and the breath, practitioners can anchor their attention in the present moment, which is a fundamental aspect of mindfulness.

Accessible to All Ages and Abilities: Mindful movement practices are generally low-impact and can be adapted to suit people of all ages and fitness levels. They are particularly beneficial for those with mobility issues or those who find sitting meditation uncomfortable.

Integrating Mindful Movement into Daily Life

To incorporate mindful movement into your meditation practice, consider the following tips:

Set Regular Times: Just as with seated meditation, consistency is key. Set aside regular times each day for your practice, and use these moments to disconnect from the busyness of daily life.

Start Small: Begin with short periods of mindful movement—just five to ten minutes can be beneficial. Gradually increase the duration as your comfort with the practice grows.

Create a Conducive Environment: While some mindful movement practices can be done anywhere, it can be helpful to practice in a quiet, clutter-free space where you are unlikely to be disturbed.

Use Guidance: For beginners, guided sessions through apps or classes can be very helpful to ensure proper technique and to enhance the meditation experience.

Reflect on Your Practice: After each session, spend a few minutes in stillness, reflecting on your practice and the sensations in your body. This can deepen the integration of physical and mental awareness.

Mindful movement practices offer a dynamic way to experience meditation. By combining movement with mindfulness, these practices not only enhance physical health but also promote mental clarity and emotional stability. Whether through walking meditation, tai chi, or gentle yoga, mindful movement is a valuable addition to traditional meditation practices, providing a holistic approach to health and well-being.

"The practice of meditation is a declaration of dignity; it asserts that our inner peace is worth cultivating. Every session is a step toward reclaiming the spaces of calm and serenity that belong inherently to us."

ppp

NINETEEN

Maintaining a Lifelong Meditation Practice

Meditation is a journey that offers continuous growth, insight, and enrichment. However, maintaining a lifelong meditation practice can be challenging amidst the shifts and changes of daily life. Over time, motivation can wane, obstacles can arise, and one might even question the value of continuing. Yet, the benefits of sustained meditation are profound and far-reaching, impacting mental, emotional, and physical health.

Establishing a Strong Foundation

The first step in sustaining a long-term meditation practice is to establish a strong foundation. This involves understanding the basic principles of meditation, finding a particular style or technique that resonates with you, and recognizing the reasons why you meditate. These reasons might include reducing stress, finding peace, enhancing concentration, or fostering a deeper sense of self-awareness. Keeping these motivations clear in your mind can serve as a powerful incentive to continue.

Routine and Consistency

The cornerstone of any enduring meditation practice is routine. Set a specific time and place for your meditation each day. This helps to establish a habit that becomes an integral part of your daily routine. Consistency is key—even if it's just for a few minutes each day. Over time, this consistency will help deepen your practice and make it a natural part of your life, just like eating or sleeping.

Setting Realistic Goals

Setting realistic, achievable goals can help maintain your motivation. These might include meditating for a certain length of time each day, gradually increasing the duration of sessions, or mastering a specific meditation technique. Celebrate small achievements along the way, and adjust your goals as your practice evolves and as your needs change.

Incorporating Variety

While consistency in the time and place of meditation is beneficial, incorporating variety in the methods or types of meditation can keep the practice fresh and engaging. If you usually practice concentration meditation, try integrating mindfulness or loving-kindness meditation into your routine. Attending meditation retreats, workshops, or classes can also introduce new perspectives and techniques, revitalizing your interest and commitment.

Community Support

Joining a meditation group or community can provide encouragement, support, and motivation. Practicing with others offers a sense of camaraderie and accountability, which can be especially helpful when your personal motivation is low. Sharing experiences and challenges with fellow meditators can provide insights and solutions that reinvigorate your practice.

Dealing with Plateaus and Setbacks

Every long-term practice encounters plateaus, where progress seems to stall, or setbacks, where circumstances disrupt regular practice. When faced with these challenges, it's important to be patient and kind to yourself. Revisit your motivations for meditating, adjust your practice if necessary, and remember that meditation is a journey with ups and downs. Sometimes, simply returning to the basics and focusing on the simplicity of breathing can help overcome these hurdles.

Integrating Meditation into Daily Life

To keep your meditation practice alive, look for opportunities to integrate mindfulness into everyday activities. This could mean practicing mindful eating, walking, or even listening. The more you integrate the principles of meditation into your daily life, the more ingrained the practice will become.

Educating Yourself Continually

The field of meditation is vast and deeply nuanced. Continually educating yourself about new meditation research, techniques, and philosophies can provide ongoing inspiration. Books, podcasts, and courses are great resources that can keep your practice intellectually stimulating and emotionally rewarding.

Renewal Through Teaching

If you have been practicing meditation for a long time, consider teaching others. Sharing your knowledge and experiences can renew your own enthusiasm for the practice. Teaching is also a powerful way to deepen your understanding of meditation, as it challenges you to articulate concepts and techniques clearly and thoughtfully.

Maintaining a lifelong meditation practice is a rewarding endeavor that requires flexibility, commitment, and a willingness to adapt. By establishing a routine, setting realistic goals, seeking out community support, and continually finding ways to integrate and renew your practice, you can enjoy the profound benefits of meditation throughout your life. As you grow and change, so too can your meditation practice, becoming an ever-evolving source of strength, peace, and insight.

ᏜᏜᏜ

"Meditation is not an escape from reality but an approach to it with a new perspective. It offers us the tools to face life's challenges with a calm mind and a compassionate heart. With these tools, every challenge becomes an opportunity for growth."

ᐯᐯᐯ

TWENTY

REFLECTIONS AND MOVING FORWARD: THE CONTINUOUS JOURNEY OF MEDITATION

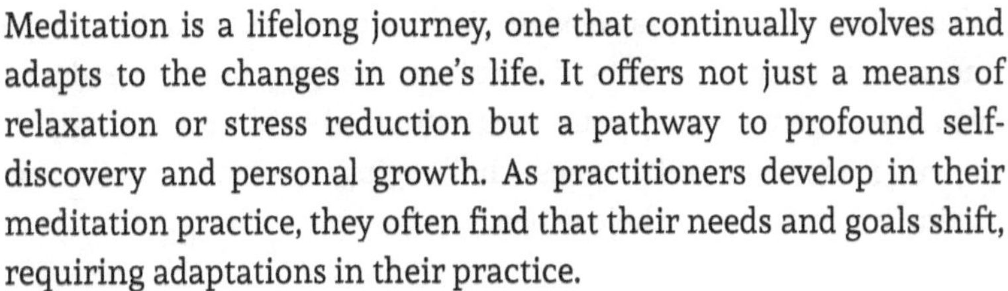

Meditation is a lifelong journey, one that continually evolves and adapts to the changes in one's life. It offers not just a means of relaxation or stress reduction but a pathway to profound self-discovery and personal growth. As practitioners develop in their meditation practice, they often find that their needs and goals shift, requiring adaptations in their practice.

The Importance of Reflection in Meditation

Reflection is a critical component of deepening one's meditation practice. It involves looking back on your experiences, understanding the changes that have occurred within you, and recognizing the benefits that have unfolded over time. Reflective practice can help you see how meditation affects your reactions to stress, your relationships, and your overall sense of well-being. Keeping a meditation journal can be an excellent way to track these reflections, allowing you to see patterns and growth over time.

Embracing Continuous Growth

Meditation is not a static practice but a dynamic one that grows with you. Continuous growth in meditation is about being open to exploring new techniques, deepening your understanding of the practice, and consistently challenging yourself to integrate mindfulness more fully into your daily life. As you progress, you might find that practices that once worked well no longer serve you as effectively, or that your life circumstances—such as a new job, a move, or family changes—shift your needs and opportunities for meditation.

Adapting Meditation to Life's Changes

As life changes, so too can your meditation practice. Here are some strategies to adapt and continue your growth through meditation:

Adjust Your Schedule as Needed: Your daily routine might change due to a variety of factors like career changes, family needs, or even retirement. Adjust your meditation schedule accordingly. If morning meditation becomes challenging, consider meditating during lunch breaks or before bed.

Modify Your Meditation Space: Changes in your living situation might require you to create a new meditation space. Be flexible and create a space that helps you feel relaxed and undistracted, regardless of how small or temporary it might be.

Explore Different Meditation Forms: If you find that your current meditation practice is no longer fitting your needs, explore other forms. For instance, if you are dealing with physical constraints, try a more passive form of meditation like guided imagery or mindfulness meditation that does not require a strict posture.

Use Technology: If finding time for a meditation class is challenging, use technology to your advantage. Online classes, apps, and podcasts can provide guidance and support for meditation when attending a live session isn't feasible.

Incorporate Mini-Meditations: When life becomes too hectic for longer sessions, incorporate mini-meditations into your day. Even a few minutes of deep breathing or mindful walking can be beneficial.

Encouraging Resilience Through Meditation

Meditation can build resilience, equipping you to better handle the stressors of life. Regular practice cultivates a kind of mental and emotional strength that can help you face challenges with a more balanced perspective and less anxiety. Continue to use meditation not just as a tool for personal tranquility but as a means of fostering resilience.

Engaging with a Community

Engaging with a meditation community can provide support and inspiration, which is particularly valuable when you encounter obstacles in your practice or when major life changes occur. Community connections can provide emotional support, deepen your learning, and keep you motivated.

Renewing Commitment

Periodically, it's beneficial to renew your commitment to your meditation practice. Set aside time to reflect on what you have achieved and what you wish to attain moving forward. Renewing your commitment can reinvigorate your practice, help you set new intentions, and align your meditation practice with your current life situation.

As you move forward in your meditation journey, keep in mind that every session is an opportunity for growth and self-discovery. By reflecting on your progress, adapting to changes, and embracing the evolving nature of your practice, you can ensure that meditation remains a valuable and enriching part of your life. Whether you are facing new challenges or celebrating achievements, meditation can provide grounding and perspective, helping you navigate the complexities of life with greater ease and insight.

PPP

"In our deepest meditations, we discover that we are not isolated beings but threads in a grand tapestry of existence. This realization fosters an unparalleled solidarity with the universe, guiding us to act with greater purpose and understanding."

❤❤❤

TWENTY-ONE
SUMMARY

The journey through the various facets of meditation, as explored in the previous chapters, underscores its profound versatility and transformative power. Meditation, an ancient practice rooted in many cultures worldwide, offers significant benefits across all aspects of life—from enhancing personal health and emotional well-being to improving relationships and productivity in the workplace. This summary revisits the key insights from each area of meditation practice and reflects on how integrating these practices into daily life can lead to a more mindful, peaceful, and fulfilling existence.

Fundamentals and Deepening Practices

We began by exploring the basics of meditation, understanding its definition, and appreciating its rich historical significance. The initial chapters provided a foundation by introducing various meditation types and techniques, emphasizing that anyone can start meditation with just a few minutes each day. As practitioners grow in their experience, they can deepen their practice by exploring different meditation forms, attending retreats, and integrating more advanced techniques, continually evolving their practice in response to personal growth and life changes.

Meditation in Daily Life

Incorporating meditation into daily routines emerged as a recurring theme. From mindful eating to mindful walking, we discussed how meditation could transform routine activities into opportunities for mindfulness and self-awareness. Such practices not only enhance the immediate benefits of meditation but also ensure that its principles profoundly permeate one's lifestyle, leading to sustained improvements in mental focus, stress reduction, and overall life satisfaction.

Specialized Applications

Specific chapters addressed how meditation could be tailored to meet the needs of different age groups and personal circumstances, illustrating meditation's adaptability. For children, meditation can foster better focus and emotional regulation. Teenagers benefit from enhanced stress management and self-esteem, adults enjoy improved productivity and reduced workplace stress, and the elderly can find solace and improved cognitive function through tailored meditation practices.

Health and Wellness

Significant attention was given to the physical and mental health benefits of meditation. Regular practice has been shown to alleviate symptoms of stress and anxiety, manage pain, support cardiovascular health, and promote a healthier immune system. The connection between yoga and meditation highlighted how combining physical activity with meditative practices could enhance physical flexibility and mental serenity, offering a holistic approach to health that is beneficial at any age.

Community and Technological Support

The role of community in sustaining a meditation practice was also highlighted. Joining meditation groups and engaging with like-minded individuals can provide motivational support and deepen one's practice through shared experiences and collective wisdom. Additionally, we discussed how technology, through apps and online resources, can facilitate access to meditation guidance and tracking, making it easier than ever to start and maintain a regular practice regardless of one's busy schedule.

Challenges and Adaptations

Adapting meditation practices to accommodate life's various phases and challenges is crucial. Life changes, such as shifts in personal or professional responsibilities, might necessitate adjustments in how and when one meditates. Embracing flexibility in one's meditation practice, such as altering duration, time, or technique, ensures that meditation remains a supportive and enriching part of life.

Throughout this exploration, one theme remains clear: meditation is more than just a tool for relaxation—it is a pathway to a deeper understanding of oneself and a more engaged way of life. Each breath and moment of mindfulness can be a step toward greater peace and clarity. As we move forward, let us carry the lessons of meditation into every moment, using them to cultivate a life of awareness, compassion, and connection. Whether you are a novice just starting your journey or a seasoned practitioner deepening your practice, meditation offers a wellspring of benefits that can enhance every aspect of your life. By committing to regular practice and embracing the principles of mindfulness in daily activities, we can all enjoy a more balanced, peaceful, and fulfilling existence.

ﭘﭘﭘ

Citation And Reference

This book represents the culmination of extensive research and meticulous analysis, incorporating a diverse range of sources, including numerous books, scholarly studies, and personal experiences. Additionally, I have scoured various websites to gather relevant information and data essential for the compilation of this work. I have taken every precaution to ensure the accuracy of the information presented and have diligently cited all sources to acknowledge their contributions.

Despite these efforts, the possibility of inadvertent errors remains. I deeply value the insights of my readers and appreciate any feedback that can help identify and rectify such inaccuracies. I encourage you to bring any discrepancies to my attention.

Your feedback is not only welcome but crucial, as it will aid in correcting current editions and enhancing the content of future ones. I am committed to maintaining the highest standards of accuracy and reliability in my work and thank you for your support and understanding.

Additionally, I firmly uphold the principle of freedom of speech and expression as guaranteed under Article 19(1)(a) of the Constitution of India, and I respect the diverse viewpoints and expressions of all readers.

ᗡᗡᗡ

Other Books Of The Author

1. Empowering Minds: A Journey into Women's Self-Discovery and Power
2. The Dynamics of Motivation: Catalyzing Thought into Action
3. Meditation and Mental Well Being: The Path to Inner Peace and Clarity
4. The Psychology of Child Education: Nurturing Future Generations
5. Ethical Enlightenment: A Modern Guide to Living with Integrity
6. Voices of Empowerment: Stories of Women Rising Against Odds
7. Social Psychology in Everyday Life: Understanding Human Connections
8. The Essence of Motivational Speaking: Inspiring Change in Others
9. Balancing Acts: Women, Work, and the Will to Lead
10. Mindful Parenting: Raising Children with Compassion and Awareness
11. The Power of Positive Aging: Embracing Life After Fifty
12. Building Resilient Communities: Social Work in Action
13. The Ethical Educator: Principles for Teaching and Learning
14. From Insight to Impact: Social Psychology for a Better World
15. Cultivating Compassion: A Guide to Ethical Living
16. The Science of Self-Help: Navigating Life's Challenges with Psychological Wisdom
17. The Mindful Leader: Meditation Techniques for Modern Management
18. Breaking Barriers: Women's Pathways to Leadership and Empowerment
19. Educating Hearts: The Role of Emotional Intelligence in Child Development
20. Transformative Talks: Insights into Motivational Oratory
21. Green Ethics: A Path to Sustainable Living

ཕཕཕ

Contact

Dr. Minakshi Bansal
Social Activist
Ahmedabad, Gujarat, Bharat
minakshiindiag20@yahoo.com

❧❧❧

|| LOKAHA SAMASTHAHA SUKHINO BHAVANTU ||

• 133 •

|| LOKAHA SAMASTHAHA SUKHINO BHAVANTU ||